DESIGN IT!

HAIR AND MAKEUP DESIGN

Alix Wood

Gareth Stevens
PUBLISHING

Please visit our website, **www.garethstevens.com**.
For a free color catalog of all our high-quality books,
call toll free 1-800-542-2595 or fax 1-877-542-2596

Cataloging-in-Publication Data
Names: Wood, Alix.
Title: Hair and makeup design / Alix Wood.
Description: New York : Gareth Stevens Publishing, 2018. | Series: Design it! | Includes index.
Identifiers: ISBN 9781538207994 (pbk.) | ISBN 9781538207956 (library bound) | ISBN 9781538207833 (6 pack)
Subjects: LCSH: Hairdressing--Juvenile literature. | Hairstyles--Juvenile literature. | Cosmetics--Juvenile literature.
Classification: LCC TT975.W66 2018 | DDC 646.7'24--dc23

First Edition

Published in 2018 by
Gareth Stevens Publishing
111 East 14th Street, Suite 349
New York, NY 10003

Produced for Gareth Stevens by Alix Wood Books
Designed by Alix Wood
Editor: Eloise Macgregor
Projects created by Deborah Robbins
Editor for Gareth Stevens: Kerri O'Donnell

Photo credits: Cover, 10, 11, 12, 13, 14, 15, 16, 17 top and 17 bottom right, 18 bottom, 19, 20 right, 21, 23 middle and right, 24, 25, 28, 29 top © Chris Robbins Photography; 4 © St Helena/iStock; 5 top, 6, 7 top, 8, 9, 18 top right, 20 left, 29 bottom © Adobe Stock Images; 5 bottom Shutterstock; 7 bottom, 22 bottom, 26, 27 top and middle © Alix Wood; 17 bottom left © Scott Griessel/Dreamstime; 18 top left © Image Source/iStock; 22 top © Mahalo Briana; 23 bottom © McKay Savage

With grateful thanks to my models Davina Cresswell, Primrose Taylor, and Harold and Ruby Wilton.

Printed in the United States of America
CPSIA compliance information: Batch # CS17GS: For further information contact Gareth Stevens, New York, New York at 1-800-542-2595.

CONTENTS

HAIR AND MAKEUP DESIGN

Have you ever thought of being a hair and makeup designer? There are all kinds of different jobs that you can do that involve hair and makeup. It's a career that needs artistic flair and technical know-how.

Hair and makeup designers work in beauty **salons** and on film sets. Some designers specialize in one kind of makeup, such as **nail technicians**, who concentrate on nail art.

Makeup is a fun way to **accentuate** your favorite features.

Mascara is great eye makeup! You can give your lashes a makeup-free lift using eyelash curlers, too.

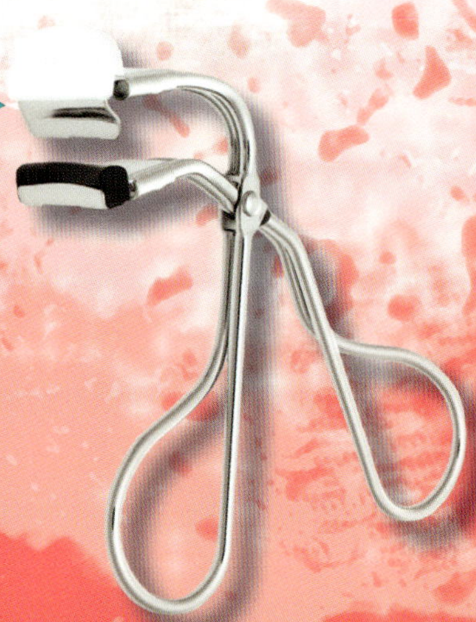

MOVIE MAKEUP

Creating hair and makeup designs on a movie set requires a lot of variety! Makeup isn't just for making a character look pretty. Designers work with the wardrobe department to get each actor to truly look the part. One minute they might be styling a leading actor's hair, the next they could be painting blood splatters on a zombie!

Start practicing your hair and makeup skills with a group of friends. It's fun to do each other's hair and experiment with makeup.

HAIR KNOW-HOW

There are so many things that you can do with your hair. It's fun to play around and develop your own individual style. Hair products can help you achieve the look that you want. Here, some styling gel helps this boy get a cool, spiky hair look. Try it yourself using special styling gel, wax, or clay.

HAIR TYPES

What is your hair like? Is it straight, wavy, kinky, or curly? Is your hair thick or fine? Hair can feel thick if each strand is thick, or if you have a lot of fine hair. Roll a strand between two fingers. You will barely be able to feel a fine hair as you roll it. Medium-thick hair will feel like a cotton thread. Coarse hair will feel hard, wiry, and possibly crunchy.

Different hair types behave in different ways, and some types are suited to certain styles. It is a good idea to look through magazines and find photographs of people with similar hair to your own. Some celebrities change their hairstyle all the time. You can find a celebrity with hair like yours and search their photographs to see which styles you'd like to try.

Some schools have policies about hair and makeup. Remember to read your school's dress code!

Design Tips

Hair looks best if it is healthy. Keep your hair clean and be careful when using products or **heat treatments**.

In this book, you'll see several different hair accessories. Here's a guide to the different accessories:

alligator clips

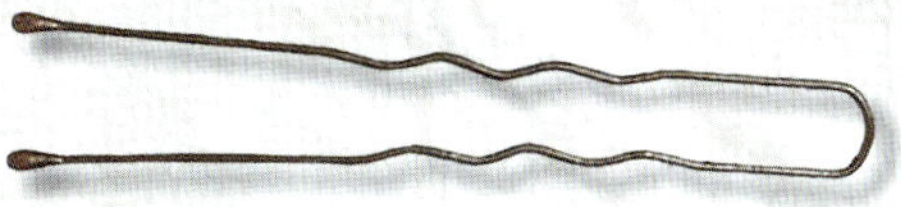

hair grips

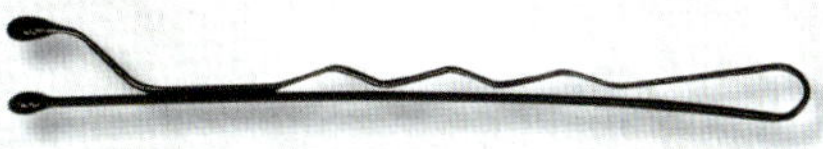

bobby pins

hair ties

SORTING THE BASICS

Keeping your skin and hair healthy is an important part of makeup and hair design. Eating a **balanced diet** full of fresh fruits and vegetables is one of the most important things you can do to keep your skin and hair healthy. All kinds of things can damage your hair. Here are some tips to help you look after your locks!

- Protect your hair from the sun by wearing a hat outside.
- The chemicals in pool water can damage hair, so wash your hair after swimming.
- Be careful when using treatments that straighten your hair and hair dyes.
- Be careful using curling irons, straighteners, and hair dryers, as they can damage your hair.

Design Tips

Dry hair can get split ends. If you look closely at the end of a hair, it will be split apart. You can't repair split ends, but you can ask a hair stylist to cut them.

SKIN CARE

It's a good idea to wash your face once or twice a day with warm water and a mild **cleanser** or soap. Always remove any makeup before you go to bed.

Bathing or showering frequently helps keep your skin healthy, too.

Exercise is good for your body in lots of ways! It gives your skin a "healthy glow." It increases blood flow to your face. Sweating also helps unclog **pores** and gets rid of oil and dirt, which helps prevent pimples. Exercise also increases blood flow to your **scalp**, keeping your hair healthy.

LIZARD HEAD

If you have short hair, try this cool lizard hair design! You will need someone to help you.

YOU WILL NEED:

- red hair chalk
- green temporary hair spray
- plastic eyes
- bobby pins
- hair clay or wax
- hair spray
- **acetate** or card stock
- scissors

1

Spike up the center section of your hair using hair clay or wax.

2

Cover your eyes and spray the spiked section green.

3

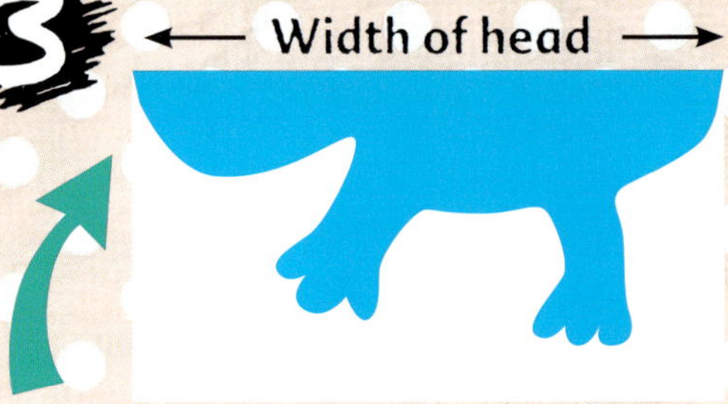

Make a **template** by drawing this blue shape on **acetate** or card stock and cutting it out.

Wear an old shirt as this will get messy! Place the lizard template on your head. Once you are happy with its position, secure it in place using bobby pins.

Check the spray can to make sure the color washes out easily! Cover your eyes. Follow the instructions on the can. Hold the template close to the hair as an adult sprays around your head. You may need someone to help hold the template.

Rub red hair chalk onto the ends of your spikes. Slide the eyes in place.

Tape each eye to a bobby pin.

NAIL ART

There are so many fun designs you can do using nail polish. It is usually best to team up with a friend and do each other's nails. The hand that you write with is a lot better at keeping steady than your other hand!

YOU WILL NEED:

- three bright colored bottles of nail polish
- a bobby pin
- some glitter
- a bowl
- nail polish remover

Nail polish drips are difficult to remove from fabric, so be careful! If your brush has too much paint on it, wipe it against the inside rim of the bottle.

1

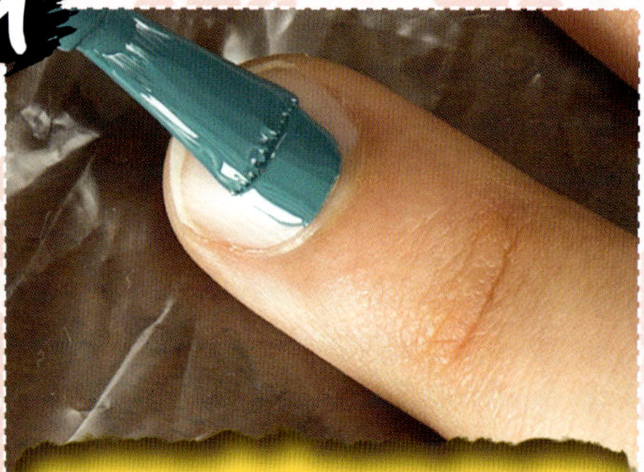

Select two very different colors that look good together, like teal and pink. Place a drop of teal polish at the bottom of the nail. Drag a little of the droplet to paint the center of the nail.

2

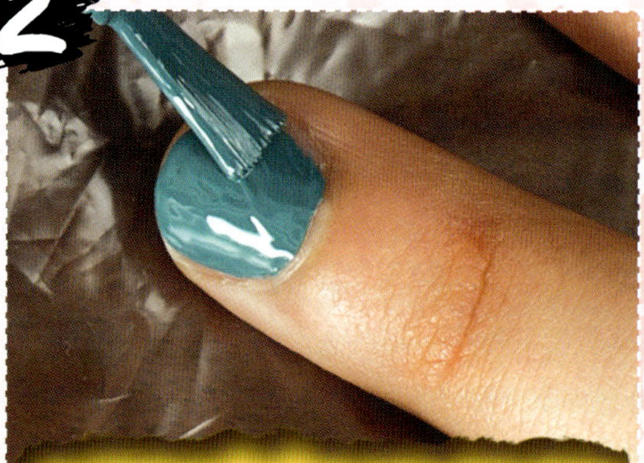

Most nail artists use three strokes to paint a nail. Using the same drop of polish, paint the sides of the nail. Try not to go over the edge. It looks best to leave a tiny gap at each edge.

3

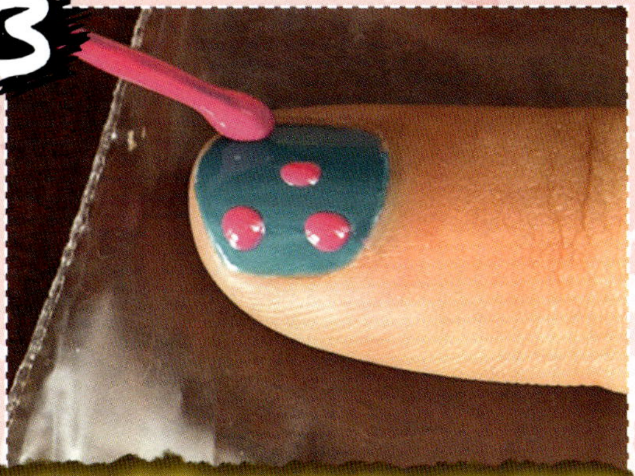

Leave the first coat of polish to dry for ten minutes. Dip the end of a bobby pin into your second color. Gently dab random spots onto your nail.

4

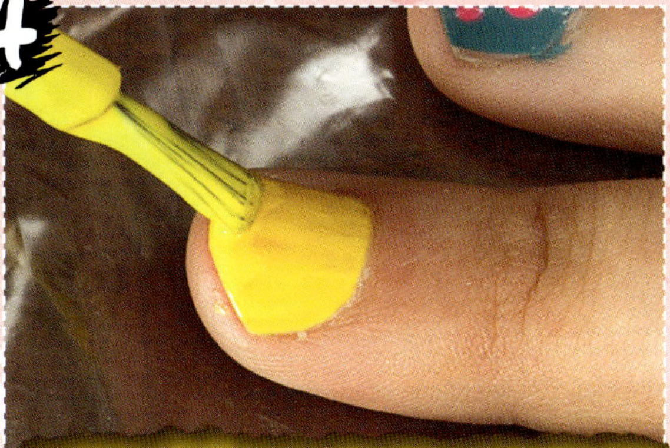

To create the glitter-tipped nails, first apply a coat of **base color** the same way as in steps 1 and 2. Once this coat is dry, dab some polish on just the tip of the nail.

5

Before your second layer dries, hold your fingers over a bowl and sprinkle glitter onto the nail. Leave for ten minutes to dry. The glitter should only stick to the tip.

Design Tips

If you do accidentally get some polish around the edges, don't worry. Clean it up using a cotton swab dipped in nail polish remover.

BIRD NEST HAIR

Does your school have a crazy hair day? If you have long hair, this is a fun style to design! You can often find little clip-on bird tree decorations around the holiday season.

YOU WILL NEED:

- a comb
- a hair tie
- some twigs and leaves
- hair pins
- clip-on birds

1

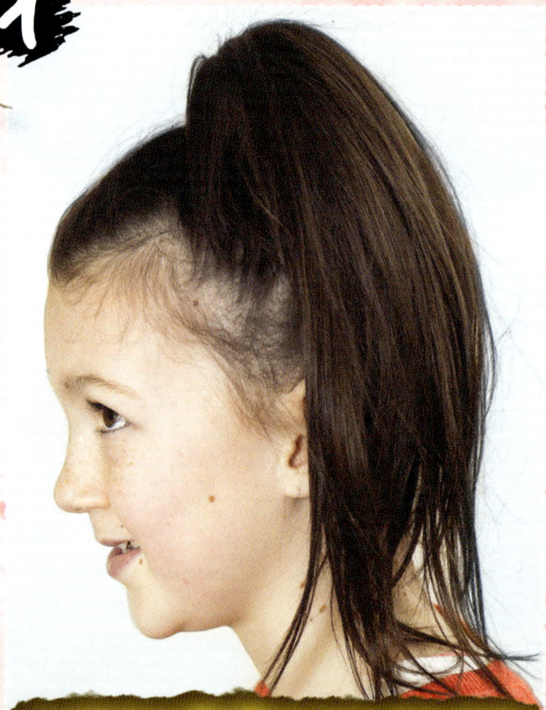

Pull the hair up into a high ponytail. It should look quite messy. You could spray on some hairspray if you have some.

2

Now **tease** the ponytail to make it look messy. Hold the ponytail up in the air. Starting near the scalp, comb the hair downward. Work your way up the ponytail until you reach the end.

3

Twist the ponytail around your hand into a bird nest shape. Tuck the end of the ponytail underneath and hold in place.

4

Pin the bird nest in place using several hair pins.

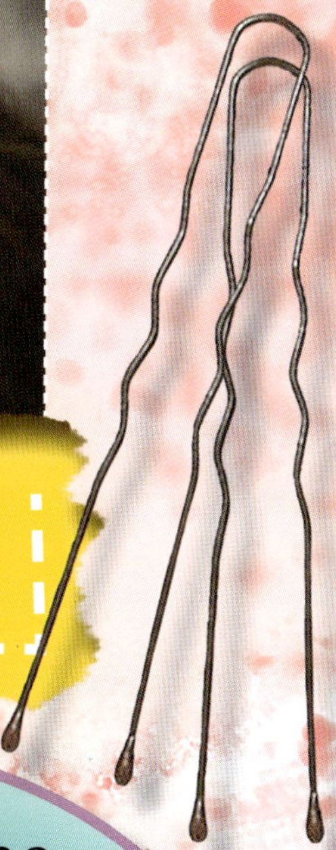

Design Tips

Pins stay in hair better if you angle them away from the center of the bun first. Then lever them over so the pins point toward the bun as you push them in.

5

Clip on your birds. Finally, push some twigs and leaves through the bun.

FACE PAINT

YOU WILL NEED:
- face paints
- makeup sponge
- thin paintbrush
- damp face cloth
- bowl of water

Makeup designers often work with face paint, creating cool designs for parties and carnivals. This Día de los Muertos (Day of the Dead) skull is easy to do and looks amazing!

Design Tips

Before you use face paint, check that you are not **allergic** to it. Try a little on the inside of your wrist and leave it for an hour.

1

Dip the sponge in the bowl. Squeeze out any **excess** water. Load the sponge with white face paint and dab it on.

2

Using a thin brush, paint black face paint in a circle around the eye. Don't get too close to the eye itself.

3

Create the little blue and red circles using a thin paint brush. Paint all the red circles first, leaving a gap between each circle. Then paint all the blue circles in the gaps.

4

Using the thin paintbrush, or an eyebrow pen, draw black lines across the lips. Draw two angle shapes under the cheekbones and a design on the forehead.

CULTURAL TRADITIONS

Some beauty and fashion designs are from specific cultures. These skull designs are based on calaveras, or sugar skulls, which are a traditional part of the Mexican holiday, Dia de los Muertos. It's important to learn about and respect the cultures that designs come from.

GLITTER AND BLING

Using glitter can really get you in the party mood. You can buy glitter eye makeup, lip gloss, and face glitter, too. If you really want to make a statement, you can even buy false eyelashes with bling!

PRIME FIRST

One makeup trick-of-the-trade is to always use a primer. You can use primer on your eyelids, face, and lips. It helps your makeup stay in place. It can also even out your skin. Primer can be clear or tinted. Choose one that matches your skin tone.

FACE GLITTER

YOU WILL NEED:

- eyeshadow
- makeup brush
- face glitter
- eyelash glue
- some sequins
- a plate

1

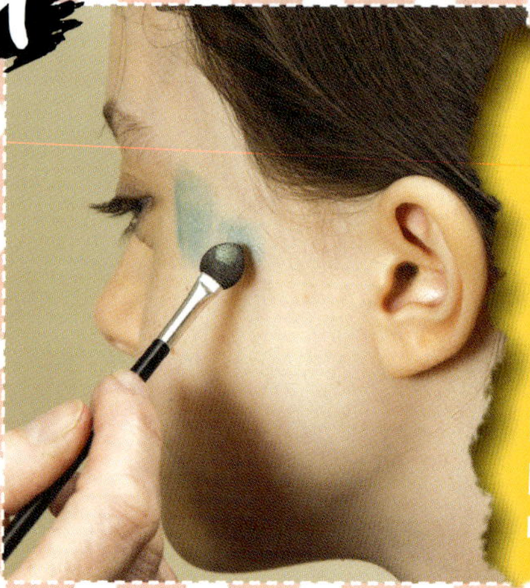

Load your makeup brush with bright eyeshadow. Draw a flower shape on the cheekbone area.

2

Dab some eyelash glue onto the flower design. Most eyelash glue contains **latex**. Check that you are not allergic to latex before you use it!

3

Hold a plate under your chin to catch the falling glitter. Shut your eyes and tip some glitter over the area where you put the glue.

4

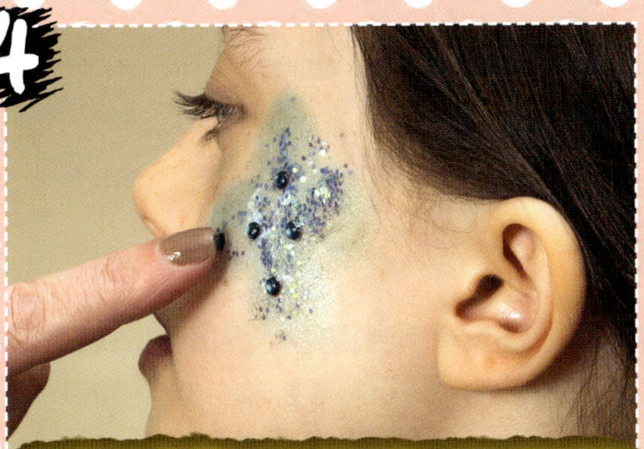

Press a few sequins in place using eyelash glue.

Design Tips

Experiment with different **color schemes** and designs. You could try making a glitter butterfly or a sparkly spiral shape.

STAGE MAKEUP

Makeup artists often work for film and TV companies. Try doing some cool stage makeup. A nasty, gaping wound can be just great for Halloween. It's pretty easy to make and looks really convincing. Creep out your friends and give it a try!

YOU WILL NEED:

- a glue stick
- a blunt butter knife
- foundation that matches your skin
- face paint
- red lip gloss

Food coloring stains, so wear old clothes if you use fake blood!

1

Smear several layers of glue stick glue on your arm using a blunt knife. Mold until it is thick in the center, and thin and smooth at the edges.

2

Let the glue harden a little. Using the blunt knife, gently drag a line through your "wound."

3

Put a small blob of the foundation on your fingertip. Gently dab the foundation onto the glue wound. Quick, gentle dabs work best. Otherwise, the glue may stick to your finger and come off.

4

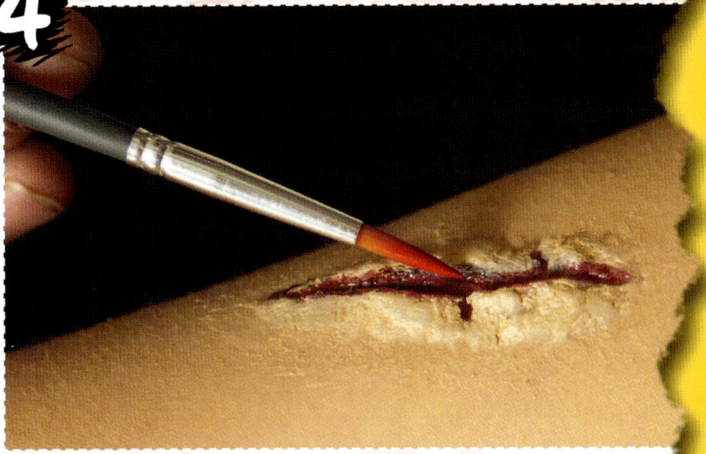

Now to add the gore! You can use red lip gloss, lipstick, and red and black face paint. First paint some red inside the wound. Add tiny touches of black around the edge of the wound. Then drip in some red lip gloss. Yuck!

FAKE BLOOD

Here's a recipe to make your own super realistic fake blood! Mix 1 cup of water with 3 cups of powdered sugar. Add a few drops of red food coloring. To make the color more realistic, mix in half a teaspoon of cocoa powder.

Design Tips

You can add some more gore to your wound by wrapping some of your arm in fake, blood-soaked bandages, like on the zombie on page 20.

MEHNDI ART

Mehndi is a form of body art from India. Elaborate patterns are painted onto the skin using **henna**. Henna is a natural dye made from the henna plant.

You can buy little cones of henna dye. You cut off the end and use the cone like a pastry bag. The dye will stain for several weeks, so you can use a liquid eyeliner instead.

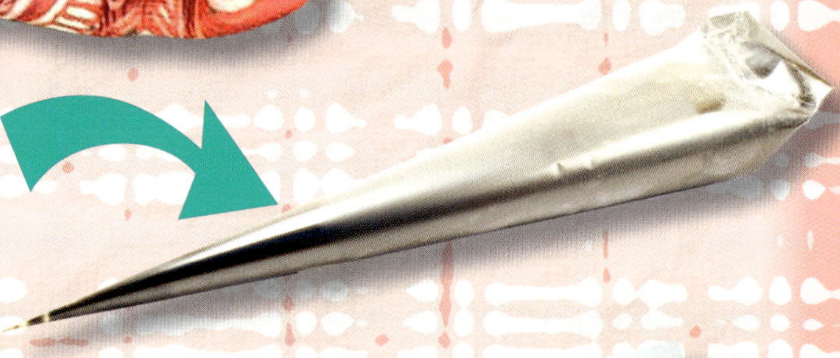

Design Tips

To practice your mehndi design, draw an outline of your hand on a piece of paper. Draw your design using pencil so you can change it if you are not happy with it. Once you like it, draw over the pencil using a ballpoint pen.

YOU WILL NEED:

- pen and paper
- a henna cone or a liquid eyeliner

1

Practice with your liquid eyeliner or henna cone on some paper before you start. Then start to draw your design on the palm.

2

Continue your design up the fingers. Liquid eyeliner will wash off quite easily with soap and water. Henna dye may stain for several weeks, though.

It can be quite ticklish drawing on your palm!

3

If you choose to use henna paste, follow the packet's instructions. You usually need to leave the paste on for a few hours and then scrape it off to reveal the dye.

HAIR WRAPS

Hair wraps are a fun way to add some color to your hair. They are pretty simple to do once you get the knack for them. It's easier to do them on someone else's hair, so pair up with a friend and have fun doing each other's wraps.

YOU WILL NEED:

- an alligator clip
- long colorful embroidery threads
- a rubber band

1

Choose an area of hair hidden by other hair. That way you will be able to hide it if you want to. Fasten back the top layer of hair using alligator clips.

2

Braid a small section of hair. It can sometimes be tricky to take the wrap out again. If the wrap is small and hidden, you can always ask an adult guardian to cut the braid off instead!

3

Choose your thread colors. Measure the threads so they are four times as long as your braid. Push three threads through the top of the braid. Pull them through until there is half the length on either side.

4

Choose a thread. Let the other threads hang down the braid. Wind your thread around the braid. Push the threads together as you wrap. To change color, just pick up a new thread.

5

If a color is running out, tie a new thread to the end of it. Tie a knot around the braid now and then to keep it secure. At the end, tie your thread in a tight double knot.

HAIR CHALKING

Using colored chalk on your hair is a great way to create some really funky hair designs. Most colors show up well on fair hair. On dark hair, use the bolder colors, such as blues, pinks, reds, and greens, for the best effect.

YOU WILL NEED:

- hair chalk
- water
- spray bottle
- old towels

1

If you want a deeper color, wet you hair first by spraying it with a water. Wear an old towel and protect the floor. Damp chalks may stain fair hair, so test a small area of hair before you chalk.

2

Twist a small section of hair. Select a hair chalk and rub it up and down the hair. Twist and untwist the hair as you rub to get more of the hair covered in the color.

3

Choose a different color chalk and select a new twisted section of hair to color.

4

You can put hair chalk anywhere on your hair. It looks really cool if you just go halfway up the hair twist. It looks as if your hair has been dipped in pots of paint!

5

Once you are happy with the colors, gently tease out the strands with your fingers. You can make the color last longer by running a curling iron through your hair, and then spraying with a light hair spray.

Design Tips

Don't use oil pastels as they will stain your hair. The chalk will suck the moisture from your hair and dry it out. Give your hair a treat by working in plenty of conditioner after you wash out your hair chalk.

EYE MAKEUP

Putting on eye makeup is all part of a hair and makeup designer's job. There are so many colors and types to choose from. The basic technique is pretty much the same, though. Try this simple eye shadow.

YOU WILL NEED:

- a makeup brush
- a dark and medium shade of the same color of eye shadow
- white eyeshadow
- mascara

1

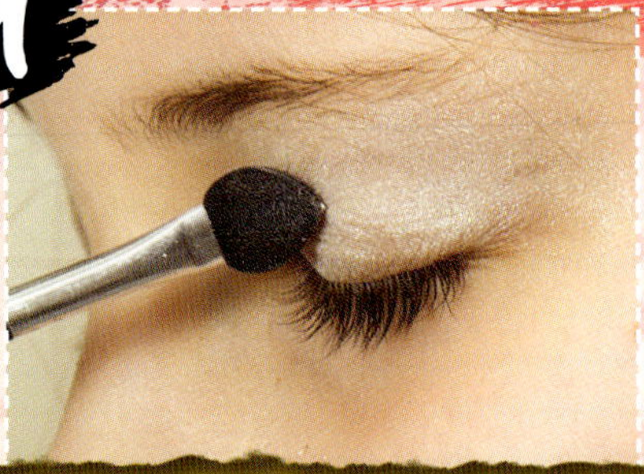

Using a makeup brush, apply the white shade on the lid and under the eyebrow.

2

Add your medium shade to the eyelid, but not in the middle area.

3

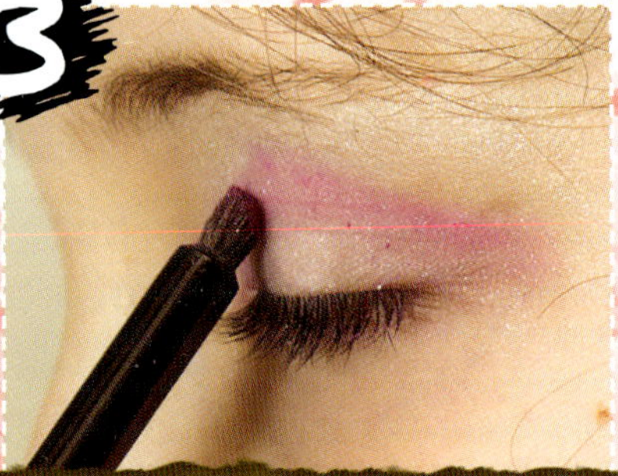

Gently bend your darkest shade into the hollow area around the eye socket.

Your shadow should look like this.

4

Put on a little mascara. Wiggle the wand slightly from side to side as you apply it.

COLOR WHEEL

What color eye shadow will you wear? A shade that contrasts with your eye color can make your eyes pop! A color wheel will help you choose a shade. Try using a color that matches your eyes, or the direct opposite color on the wheel!

Design Tips

Breaking the rules is fun too. Experiment and have fun with colors!

GLOSSARY

accentuate Emphasize.

acetate A plastic sheet.

allergic Having an abnormal reaction to substances that do not have such a strong effect on most people.

balanced diet A diet of a variety of different food providing adequate amounts of the nutrients necessary for health.

base color A first color used as a background.

braid A length of hair made up of three or more interlaced strands.

cleanser A cream for cleaning the face.

color schemes Particular combinations of colors.

excess An amount beyond what is usual, needed, or asked.

heat treatments Straightening or curling the hair using heated hair dryers or styling implements.

henna A reddish brown dye obtained from the leaves of an Old World tropical shrub and used on hair and skin.

latex A mixture of water and fine particles of rubber or plastic used especially in paints and adhesives.

nail technicians A person whose occupation is to style and shape a person's nails.

pores The tiny holes in your skin

salon A place of business for the care of customers' hair, skin, and nails.

scalp The skin and flesh of the head usually covered with hair.

tease Comb hair from the ends of the strands towards the scalp.

template A pattern used as a guide to the form of a piece being made.

FOR MORE INFORMATION

Books

Boone, Mary. *Hair Hacks: Your Tresses Troubles Solved! (Beauty Hacks)*, North Mankato, MN: Capstone Press, 2017.

Craig, Jonathan. *Special Effects Make-up Artist (The Coolest Jobs on the Planet)*, Chicago, IL: Raintree, 2015.

Websites

Check out this video to learn about the job of a Disney makeup supervisor!
https://knowitall.org/video/makeup-artist-kids-work

Learn more about being a hair stylist at this awesome site!
http://www.kidzworld.com/article/2645-becoming-a-hair-stylist

Publisher's note to educators and parents:

Our editors have carefully reviewed these websites to ensure that they are suitable for students. Many websites change frequently, however, and we cannot guarantee that a site's future contents will continue to meet our high standards of quality and educational value. Be advised that students should be closely supervised whenever they access the Internet.

INDEX